LOWRIDERS

LOWRIDERS

Ann Parr

CHELSEA HOUSE
PUBLISHERS
A Haights Cross Communications Company ®
Philadelphia

Cover Photo: George Luna's 1947 Chevrolet Sedan Delivery, christened *Midnight Illusions*, took three years to customize for the lowrider show circuit. The body of the car is lowered inches from the ground. The car is decorated with murals and features gleaming chrome.

CHELSEA HOUSE PUBLISHERS

VP, NEW PRODUCT DEVELOPMENT   Sally Cheney
DIRECTOR OF PRODUCTION   Kim Shinners
CREATIVE MANAGER   Takeshi Takahashi
MANUFACTURING MANAGER   Diann Grasse

STAFF FOR LOWRIDERS

EDITORIAL ASSISTANT Sarah Sharpless
PRODUCTION EDITOR Bonnie Cohen
PHOTO EDITOR Pat Holl
SERIES DESIGN AND LAYOUT Hierophant Publishing Services/EON PreMedia

Original edition first published in 2001.

http://www.chelseahouse.com

A Haights Cross Communications ✦ Company ®

First Printing

1   3   5   7   9   8   6   4   2

Library of Congress Cataloging-in-Publication Data

Parr, Ann.
   Lowriders / Ann Parr.
      p. cm.—(Race car legends. Collector's edition)
   Includes bibliographical references and index.
   ISBN 0-7910-8673-9
   1. Lowriders—Juvenile literature. I. Title. II. Series.
TL255.2.P368 2005
629.28'72—dc22

                                                            2005010394

All links and Web addresses were checked and verified to be correct at the time of publication. Because of the dynamic nature of the Web, some addresses and links may have changed since publication and may no longer be valid.

TABLE OF CONTENTS

1

NEW MEXICO LOWRIDERS: CLASSICS

Patrick Chavez opened the garage door. He let out a big breath. The lowrider was safe and beautiful after an early spring storm. One of these days, the *Blue Angel* would be his.

Dennis Chavez, Patrick's grandfather, said, "The day you have a high school diploma in one hand, I'll give you the keys in the other hand."[1] Four more years. Going with Grandpa to a big car show in Albuquerque had been about the best time of his life. The *Blue Angel* had placed in the Best of Show category. He was 8 years old then. He feels just as excited now.

She used to be an everyday Ford F-100 1973 pickup. But now, a red, twisted ribbon pattern on her fenders peeks through the garage windowpanes. Navy blue paint gleams with pride. Outside, in full sun, she looks sky blue, as noted by her name. Chrome rims and pipes show off the blue crushed velvet upholstery and flatbed cover. Patrick's grandmother sewed them both. Bucket seats from a Dodge van make a comfy ride. The television set stays tucked below the dash. The sunroof, open, lets in cool spring and fall breezes. Closed, it keeps out the hot Southwest heat during the

Members of a lowrider club line up to register for the Lowrider Experience car show at the Los Angeles Sports Arena in Los Angeles, California, in 2003. The show featured lowrider cars, trucks, bicycles, and such events as car hopping.

summer. From May through September, Grandpa and Patrick cruise the *Blue Angel* up and down the streets of Chimayó, New Mexico. From October to April, she takes a long winter nap, protected by fitted tarps. Little by little, Patrick's grandfather said, he changed this and added that when he had the time and money. Today, the car is one of a kind.

"I'll keep the 'Blue Angel' like it is," Patrick said. "Grandpa and I worked on it together, and it is special to me. I might add a hydraulic setup some day though."[2]

The *Blue Angel* is a lowrider. Grandpa is a lowrider, too. So is Patrick. A dictionary definition, if there were one, would call lowrider a noun: (1) a car whose body has been lowered only inches from the ground, or (2) one who drives such a car.

Chimayó, population 2,900, has at least 50 finely detailed lowriders. They are fixed up and ready to win car shows. Thirty more lowriders are called primers, a dull gray look. "That doesn't mean the rest of the car is unfinished, though,"

Artist Arthur "Lolo" Medina of Chimayó, New Mexico, is shown washing his lowrider. Medina has decided to adorn his 1976 Cadillac with religious images and name it *Lowrider Heaven*. Many lowriders express their faith through religious icons displayed on their vehicles.

Patrick said. "It probably has a hydraulic setup and a nice interior."[3]

Dr. Benito Cordova, former lowrider consultant to the Smithsonian Institution, believes lowriding may have started in the eighth century. The Moors civilization in Spain led all of Europe in art, science, and commerce. People from Spain, influenced by the Moors, showed up in New Mexico during the late 1500s. They rode decorated horses—leather-tooled saddles and bridles, silver trim, draped with garlands of roses. Riders' clothing matched the horses' gear, making horse and rider look like one. "Lowriders are like modern-day ***caballeros* (horsemen)**," Dr. Cordova continued, "except that they don't ride elaborately decorated horses, they drive elaborately decorated cars."[4]

Did you know the image of the Virgin of Guadalupe is often seen on Mexican Americans' cars?

According to tradition, the Virgin Mary appeared to a young Aztec boy named Juan Diego outside Mexico City. She directed him to tell the Catholic bishop to build a church in her honor so that she could give love, hope, and protection to all Mexican people. When the bishop demanded proof of Juan's vision, the boy returned. The Virgin appeared again and gave Juan a sign—bunches of fragrant red roses suddenly blooming on the hill where cactus had grown before. Juan gathered the flowers into his cloak.

As Juan unwrapped the flowers for the bishop, an image appeared on the boy's cloak. It was the face of the Virgin Mary. Convinced that Juan was indeed delivering a holy message, the leaders of the Catholic Church built a magnificent cathedral. The image from Juan's cloak, know as the Miraculous Portrait, hangs in the cathedral, called Our Lady of Guadalupe. It is in Mexico City.

Mexicans and Mexican Americans joyfully celebrate December 12, the day that the Virgin of Guadalupe revealed herself to Juan. People bring masses of brightly colored flowers to private and public shrines. Followers trust the Virgin Mary to help, cure, and protect them, just as she promised.*

*Jacqueline Orsini Dunnington, *Viva Guadalupe!* (Santa Fe, NM: Museum of New Mexico Press, 1997).

By 1846, Mexico was not so peaceful. It disagreed with the United States about the location of the Texas border. The United States also wanted to purchase more Mexican territory, which later became the states of California, New Mexico, and Arizona. These differences led to the Mexican-American War, a bloody conflict that ended in 1848. Many Mexicans did not recognize the takeover of the land by the United States. They wanted their own ways and their own land.

For most of Mexico's history, only a few people controlled the country's power and wealth. The majority of Mexico's citizens lived in poverty. Francisco Madero, educated in Europe and the United States, led some strikes against General Porfirio Diaz, Mexico's leader. By 1910, Diaz was pressured into holding an election. Madero gained many votes and called for a revolt against Diaz's government. November 10 is Revolution Day, a Mexican holiday celebrating the day Madero declared himself president.

Following the Mexican Revolution of 1910, many Mexicans moved to the United States. Most settled in their former territory, now within the borders of the states of Texas, California, and New Mexico, known to them as *Altzan*. They brought their ideas, customs, religious beliefs, and art with them. Even today, lowriders from New Mexico display something about that time in Mexico's history.

Cruising in New Mexico and elsewhere may be the remains of an old courtship ritual brought to the United States by Mexicans. Young, unmarried people would walk around the central plaza of a town, women in one direction and men in the opposite direction. Lowriders do something similar. They circle the plaza, look at each other's cars, and return home to talk about what they saw.

Española, a few miles from Chimayó, is famous for its history of cruising, too. This town of 9,600 people has

A painting of the Virgin of Guadalupe, the most loved and revered of all saints in Mexico, is featured on the side of this lowrider in Santa Fe, New Mexico. Jacqueline Orsini Dunnington, who has documented and photographed the lowrider phenomena, coined the term "Rolling Temple" to describe a lowrider that features a religious icon.

more customized cars than regular cars. Tomas Martinez, an Española banker and founder of the Vicious Dreams lowrider club, says lowriders in Española are definitely family-oriented.

"We have had as many as 6,000 people show up for our mid-August Super Show with more than 300 car entries," Tomas said. "Working on a lowrider for a show pulls families together."[5] Shows like this one make large amounts of money that are used for schools and community projects.

Cruising in Española and Chimayó is common on the weekends during the spring and summer. Some lowriders drive to Taos or Santa Fe. "When we get to Taos, we set up a nice cruise on the Main Plaza," Dennis Chavez, Patrick's grandfather, said. "I tell lowriders to stay on the right. Take your time. Don't block both lanes. It gets you in trouble with the police. Besides, people can't see you, and then you've missed the point."[6]

Patrick is part of the low and slow way of life in Chimayó. Grandmothers, teenagers, and even city council members cruise the streets in sparkling cars painted with artistic murals showing the driver's ideas about family, history, and memories. Lowriders dress up Chimayó's and Española's streets and countryside, just as the decorated horse and rider did so long ago. "It's all about honoring our culture," Patrick says. "My grandmother's side and my grandfather's side of the family all get together with other families who go to car shows. We cruise to the country, set up the cars, pull out some chairs, walk around to look at the cars, and eat a big lunch. It's a family thing."[7]

②
CALIFORNIA AND TEXAS LOWRIDERS

Beginning in the 1920s, California car owners fixed up their car engines to race the wide Los Angeles streets. Louver doors to cool the racing engines decorated the sides of the cars. Some owners chopped through the tops and lowered the front ends of their cars to make them go faster. They liked the look of these changes. They called their cars hot rods.

On the east side of Los Angeles, where Mexican immigrants lived, each family could not afford its own car. Cars were often owned by groups of families. Like the hot rods on the other side of Los Angeles, these owner-families lowered their cars. But they lowered the back ends too by putting sandbags in the trunk or cutting the suspension coils. They wanted their own customized look. They wanted to be noticed when cruising down the streets, not racing.

Just as the attire of the rider and horse matched centuries earlier, these *pauchucos* (young Mexican Americans) dressed in a distinctive style, too. They wore zoot suits—thigh-length jackets worn over trousers that were wide at the top and narrow at the bottom, called pegged legs. The *pauchucos* often put slim crosses around their necks and spongy-soled, shiny

In the 1940s, young Mexican Americans in East Los Angeles adopted the zoot suit as part of their unique style.

black shoes on their feet. A gleaming slicked-back hairdo finished the look. (Elvis Presley adopted this style years later.)

By the 1950s, a booming Los Angeles automotive industry had become the second largest producer of cars and tires in the United States. Mexican Americans worked in the factories where they learned about building cars. They used these acquired skills to customize their own cars.

Whittier Boulevard in East Los Angeles was the place Mexican Americans cruised to show off their customized cars. It was a place to meet and stay together, a way to communicate with each other, and a way to preserve their culture. Groups would borrow someone's house for a Saturday night. They would cruise Whittier, announcing where the party was. Party-goers paid $5 for food and live music. Groups made money this way. They used it to pay for college costs, to help others fix their cars, or to pay someone's bills. Cruising got people involved and committed to supporting each other, having a nice car, and dressing nicely. These groups became informal car clubs for Mexican Americans.

Many cruisers referred to themselves as Chicanos. Some clung to the idea that the United States took land from Mexico. They believed that the treaty at the end of the

Lowriders cruise in a scene from *Boulevard Nights*. The movie depicts Chicano lowriders as gang members and criminals, a negative stereotype that lowriders strive to overcome.

Mexican American War in 1910 was illegal and immoral. As Chicanos learned more about government, they told their friends and families how their taxes paid the sheriffs who forced them off Whittier. Taxes also paid for maintenance of their streets. They learned about the right to peaceful assembly (meeting together on Whittier Boulevard).

Chicanos, now better informed, wanted to improve relations with Los Angeles law officials. They removed graffiti from walls and maintained the Boulevard as much as possible. Newspaper, radio, and television coverage was thorough and helpful. Police were invited to special meetings. Sometimes the Chicanos and the police could work

Lowriders show off their customized vintage cars at Stearns Wharf, a popular meeting place in Santa Barbara, California.

out acceptable rules for cruising. Other times they couldn't. Throughout the years, lowriders and law enforcement have been both friends and enemies.

The lowrider movement in California had its ups and downs, but it continued to grow in spite of setbacks. Then a movie, *Boulevard Nights*, released in 1979, showed lowriders as gang members, criminals, and a negative influence on society. Law enforcement, especially in California, reacted as

 **how the word *lowrider* first came into use?**

During the 1960s, the Vietnam War caused tension between races of people in the United States. Dissatisfaction with the Civil Rights Act of 1964 that promised equal opportunities made things worse. On August 11, 1965, a white Los Angeles police officer pulled over an African-American driver. The officer thought the driver was drunk. While police questioned the man and his brother, a crowd gathered. The boys' mother arrived. Police arrested all three family members, using batons to overpower the brothers, angering the gathering crowd. Tensions boiled over, and rioting began. The rioting lasted for 6 days, killing 34 people and injuring more than 1,000. An estimated $100 million in damage was done to property.

During the searches and arrests, some owners of cruisers removed the seats from their cars. They and their passengers stayed hidden from authorities and others who wanted to harm them. The public began to refer to these cars as *lowriders*, because the riders could not be seen. The word started as an uncomplimentary term for the young African Americans accused of causing trouble. But some liked the new word. Soon, even those with the best cars and highest intentions started calling themselves lowriders. The press also began to talk about lowriders. The name, intended as an insult, stuck as a name for lowered cars and their owners.

if all lowriders were bad. Cruising in California hit a slump. But lowriders did not give up.

California lowriders say they have set the pace of the lowrider movement since it began. They pushed the limits with lawmakers, engineers, painters, and designers. They maintained a special style all their own. Some call it wild and crazy. Some call it evil. Some see it as very creative.

Others say that the lowriders who originated in Texas as *pauchucos* first made their way from Mexico to the United States. As early as the 1940s, lowered cars cruised the Texas border about the same time serious riders showed up in New Mexico and California. By the mid-1960s, cruisers were commonly seen in San Antonio, Del Rio, Dallas, Fort Worth, and El Paso.

Armando Santillan tells his story of moving from East Los Angeles to El Paso in 1970. When he and members of his Exclusives Club saw a 1964 Chevrolet Impala painted black with a charcoal-gray top, they decided to paint all their cars black and gray. One member couldn't afford a car, but he had a hearse. As they cruised toward El Paso's finest lowrider park, they lined up, with the hearse last. Two police officers mistook them for a funeral procession. The police escorted the cruisers, stopped traffic for them, and followed them to the lowrider park. When the police realized what was going on, they issued tickets to the lowriders for stopping traffic. The club went to court, pleaded innocent, and won their case. They decided to give their club a new name—the Undertakers.

Everybody has reasons for lowriding. California lowriders like to cruise, be seen, and be known for their wild, sleek, new designs. They want to win shows and prizes. Texas lowriders want to win trophies at car shows, too, but it is not their main motivation. Texas lowriders are quiet and independent

The plush interior of this lowrider is displayed at a car show. Owners take pride in expressing their vision and sharing their culture through the lowrider tradition.

about their lowriding. They view their cars as big canvases where they perform their artwork. The interior is like the comfort of their homes. The trim on the inside and the outside shows the owner's pride. However, both California and Texas share the first reason for lowriding—to be seen and to share their culture.

③
CREATION OF A LOWRIDER

Anyone can be a lowrider. Anyone can create a lowrider. Cars, trucks, motorcycles, bicycles, tricycles, and even model cars can become lowriders. Putting the vehicle closer to the ground makes it a lowrider. Any customizing after that is left to the owner's imagination.

Owners do as much of the work as possible. They help each other, too. They share knowledge, they share tools, and they share ideas. Lowriding has always been a community affair—a way to share the culture. When outside help is needed, other lowriders know the best places.

Lona and Sons of Kansas City, Missouri, is the only full-time lowrider shop in the area. "My grandfather started as Lona Brothers Garage in 1942," Tim Lona said. "Through several evolutions, we became Lona and Sons Hydraulics and Lowriders in 1995." Tim and Chris work with their father, Charlie.

Tim Lona began working on hydraulic setups in the 1980s. His first lowrider was a 1964 Chevrolet Impala. Tim said, "I took my car to shows until I finally killed it in 1997. I had hopped and danced it so much, it just sprawled out and died!"[8] Tim now owns and works on a 1971 Chevrolet Impala sport coupe and a 1975 Chevrolet Caprice convertible.

"We have a good product, we do good work, and we maintain good customer relations," Tim said. "One car we worked on delivered Eddie Gorerro, the wrestler, into the ring in Wichita, Kansas, recently."[9] Lona and Sons makes their own brand of hydraulic setups called the Wicked Series. They make some of the parts in Kansas City; others are ordered from China. Lona and Sons specializes in hydraulic setups only.

Putting a car down—lowering it—means making one of several choices. In the 1940s, local muffler shops would heat the springs and melt some of the coils away for a small price of $5. That would be enough—an altered suspension system—and it was a lowrider. Ready to cruise on Sunday afternoons, the car was brought down as close to the ground as possible.

Driving a lowered car was not easy. Cars scraped the streets, hit all the bumps, and sparks flew. Besides, were they safe? Many law officials thought not. By 1959, California had passed laws prohibiting vehicles to operate with any part of the car below the lowest part of the wheel rim. With even the smallest tires, cars that were legal were still 5-1/2 inches off the ground. That was too high for most lowriders. "I didn't want to raise my car," Ray Aguirre of East Los Angeles said, "but I had too many tickets."[10]

Ray and his father, Louis, headed for the junk yard where old airplanes were dumped. They picked out hydraulics parts left over from B-52 bombers and rigged a system for Ray's 1957 Corvette named "X-Sonic." They changed the 24-volt machinery to 12 volts, created lowering blocks, and cut the coils. It took time to work out the details. But soon, Ray could raise the car a few inches to cruise it legally and lower it to look good when parked.

Ray led a group of cars to a 1959 Memorial Day car show in Long Beach, California. "The motorcycle cop cut across the center divider and made a U-turn, pulling us all over," Ray remembered. "By the time he got to me, I had raised the car up to legal height."

"I could have sworn this car was too low," the officer said. He had carefully measured the car's clearance.

"It's the style," Ray replied. "It looks like it's really low."

As the officer returned to the other side of the freeway, Ray lowered the car again. The officer turned around, rubbed his eyes, and waved the caravan through, unsure why the club's members were laughing.

Ray used his new hydraulic setup again as the cars cruised into the auditorium. "There was a concrete barrier around the track that had to be cleared," Ray explained. "Car owners had to block their cars up to clear that barrier—except me. I drove my car up to the barrier, pushed the button to raise the car, and drove over the concrete. Well, you wouldn't believe the cheers and commotion when I did that."[11]

Others wanted to know his secret. The Aguirres searched for more parts and equipment. They soon set up a hydraulic business. The new idea grew. By 1980, some cars could flip over with their high-powered systems, or drivers could lift each corner of the car by itself. Cars danced, turned in circles, jumped over barriers, and hopped from one place to another. Hydraulic cylinders, chromed, sat next to batteries lined up in trunks and under floorboards. The new idea had taken hold. By 1981, the *hop*, or how high a car could jump,

This car is participating in a hopping contest. Hydraulics were introduced so owners could raise or lower cars with the flick of a switch. A hydraulics system also enables a vehicle to jump, buck, and hop.

was the most popular category at car shows. To enter the hop contest, a car must jump at least 21 inches off the ground.

Throughout the years, builders added new ideas to hydraulics technology. Truck beds turned in circles with a new scissors lift. Speed and height records were made and broken at shows. Only the top builders guessed what the limits might be.

Like Raul Aguirre so many years ago, many lowriders use hydraulic systems with oil pressure pumps and cylinders. Owners remove the springs and front shock absorbers from the cars. They replace the shocks with cylinders. The cylinders are connected to hydraulic pumps, usually

Not all cars can take the strain of car hopping. This wheel collapsed after the car bounced too hard in a hopping contest sponsored by *Lowrider* magazine in Los Angeles, California in 1996.

placed in the trunk. Batteries power the pumps to push fluid into the cylinders, which lift the vehicle's body. To lower the car, the driver flips a switch to the same pump, draining fluid from the cylinders. The car comes down.

Another way to change a suspension system is to torch, or burn, the coil springs on the wheels to a lower position. This is a permanent change, and vehicles done this way are for cruising only. There are no high speeds, no bumps, no jumping, no messing around of any kind. Owners drive these lowriders slowly, show them off proudly, and protect them carefully. "This was the 1950s way to make it low," Dennis Chavez says. "It's a sure thing. No upkeep, no repair, no problems with cylinders or switches. That's how I did my truck, the *Blue Angel*, the one that will be Patrick's."[12]

The most modern way to put a car down is air bag suspension. Adam Diaz at Master Customs Image specializes in air suspension. "We have developed a way to put air on big vehicles that does minimum alteration to the all-wheel-drive mechanism," he said. "With air, we don't cut the car, there is absolutely no maintenance required, and the ride is great compared to the rough ride with oil. Too many times, I've

This lowrider on display features chrome grillwork, engine parts, and undercarriage. Customizing a vehicle with surface chrome is a sure way to draw attention, but many owners also chrome hidden engines and undercarriages simply because they like to.

heard about pumps and cylinders coming apart, spraying oil everywhere—even fires. Air is reliable, and safe."[13]

Bringing a car down makes it a lowrider. However, owners seldom are satisfied with only a lowered look. They think about what their cars mean to them. They check out other cars and decide what to do next. For a quick, dazzling effect, chrome is a popular choice. No part of the car is off limits to chrome. Chrome wheel rims highlight the small wheels and shine brightly as the vehicle slowly cruises the roads

Did you know **lowriders make a good subject for school reports?**

Francisco Peña needed a topic for a speech class assignment. "I wanted to do something different, and I had just gotten into lowriding," he said. "So I had this idea about hydraulic systems. Have my car club friends bring their lowriders, demonstrate, and then talk about how to set up hydraulic systems. My teacher thought it was a good idea."*

On the day of the presentation, Francisco and his friends blocked off a section of the parking lot, set up a table with lowrider literature, including a hydraulic kit with cylinders, pumps, and motors. When the time came for the one-minute "show," a friend turned on loud music. For a full minute, two demonstration lowriders bucked, bounced, jumped, and hopped. Students clapped, screamed, and danced. More students poured out of classroom doors and windows to check out all the noise. By the time Francisco got to the informative part of the speech, he had a huge audience.

Francisco talked about how Raul Aguirre used airplane parts to make his car go up and down. The rest of Francisco's speech concerned cylinders, pumps, and hoses. At the end of his presentation, students wanted to get into the demonstration cars to feel the hop and jump of a lowrider. Francisco's speech was a hit, and he got an A for his efforts.

*Ann Parr's telephone interview with Francisco Peña, November 26, 1999.

or parks on a Sunday afternoon. Chrome on fenders, around bumpers and mirrors, and highlighting the grill, trunk, and hood shows off a car. Chrome on the undercarriage and on engine parts makes a snappy impression as well. Some owners dress up every part of the engine under the hood with gold- or silver-plate. Most who have done that much to their vehicles drive them only when necessary.

4
FAMOUS LOWRIDERS

Throughout the years, lowriders have become famous for various reasons. Some have unique features. Others, like Patrick Chavez's family's *Blue Angel*, are handed from one generation to the next. Some have won important prizes.

One of the world's most famous lowriders is a 1969 Ford LTD. Dave Jaramillo of Chimayó, New Mexico, its original owner, had a dream for his car when he bought it from an uncle. He flared the fenders, installed a larger V-8 engine, and added a console with bar and television. He added a sun-roof, chrome exhaust pipes, custom grill, and recessed tail-lights lined with removable velvet covers. But in 1978, Dave was killed in a pickup truck accident only 6 months after he bought the car. His wife, Irene, and his nephew, Dennis Martinez, continued Dave's work. They used candy-apple-red crushed velvet upholstery to cover the seats and trunk and engine compartments. Ribbons painted orange and pink danced on the sides and hood of the car. A black coat beneath eight layers of metal flake and at least 15 layers of candy-apple-red paint covered the car, just as Dave had planned. They named it *Dave's Dream*. The car won Best of Lowrider regional and national awards at car shows throughout New Mexico from 1979 to 1982. When Irene remarried, the car went into storage.

Dave's Dream, on exhibit at the Smithsonian National Museum of American History, began as a 1969 Ford LTD in Chimayo, New Mexico.

Dr. Lonn Taylor, historian at the Smithsonian Institution, had seen *Dave's Dream* at the Museum of New Mexico. He called Dr. Benito Cordova, his assistant. "You may think I'm crazy, but I want you to find a car I saw 10 years ago," Dr. Taylor said.[14]

Dr. Cordova bristled. He had grown up in a middle-class Hispanic neighborhood where lowriders meant gangs and crime. "I only knew about *cholos* (Mexican gangsters) who fixed up their cars to use them as weapons in traffic."[15]

But he had an assignment, and within 45 minutes, Dr. Cordova called Dr. Taylor. "It's in a garage about 3 miles from my home."[16] Dr. Cordova would soon change his mind about lowriders.

The Smithsonian Institution bought *Dave's Dream*, which, by then, had been in storage for 10 years. More than

Rap artist Snoop Dogg's (Calvin Broad) Lakers car, a 1967 Pontiac Parisienne, was custom-built by Big Slice (Michel Rich) and features hydraulics which allow it to move up and down. Big Slice also customized a bus so that Snoop, who coaches his son's football team, could transport the team in style.

75 people—family, friends, Los Bajitos Car Club members—worked with Dr. Taylor, Dr. Cordova, and the Smithsonian for 2 years restoring the car to Irene's satisfaction. A mural of the family decorated the left rear fender. A booming stereo was added. A hydraulic setup lifted and lowered the front and back ends and rocked the car from side to side. Tiny paintings filled the inside fender wells. "There's not a square inch of this car that's not painted or chromed," Dr. Taylor's boss said.[17]

Before *Dave's Dream* left Chimayó, Father C. Roca at the famous Sancturio de Chimayó church, blessed the car at a dedication ceremony. The Jaramillo family, car club members, and friends read poetry, sang, and danced. Gallons of

The hydraulics system of Snoop Dogg's lowrider sits next to an assortment of speakers in the trunk.

holy water christened the car as they turned it over to the Smithsonian. On June 24, 1992, *Dave's Dream* went on permanent display in the American History Museum at the Smithsonian Institution. Dr. Cordova believes that *Dave's Dream* may be the only lowrider to be finally finished.

Gypsy Rose, a 1964 Chevrolet Impala owned by Jesse Valdez is another famous lowrider. It shows off 150 pink, red, and white roses, totaling more than 2,500 painted petals. Jesse shaved the door handles and emblems, added a donut chain-link steering wheel, and installed a hydraulic setup.

When production of the television show *Chico and the Man* began in 1974, NBC network executives asked Jesse if they could borrow his car. They wanted to use it for opening scenes on the show. Jesse said yes. Soon, viewers who watched *Gypsy Rose* cruise onto the show every week,

Did you know all races and colors of people are lowriders?

Steve Miller of Placentia, California, is not Mexican American. He is white. He is glad all races of people are welcome to be lowriders. He first owned a 1969 Volkswagen Beetle, which he lowered and made fancy with a black leather interior. Steve painted the exterior burgundy and chrome-plated the wheels and engine parts. "It was beautiful," he says, "but I got it mostly to have fun. Then I sold it and decided to get more serious."*

Purchasing a 1995 Honda Civic, Steve set a specific goal. He wanted his car, the *Viridian Cruiser*, to be featured on the cover of *Lowrider Euro* magazine. He added air-ride suspension, custom rims, and a slide ragtop. He created an interior of yellow and blue-green to compliment the red exterior.

Steve won trophies at all the shows he entered. *Lowrider Euro* magazine took notice. The *Viridian Cruiser* was featured in the Winter 1999 issue. Having reached one goal, what was next for Steve? He sold the car and used the money to buy another car and set himself another goal.

*Ann Parr's telephone interview with Steve Miller, October 4, 1999.

began asking questions. What is this car? How do I get one? NBC helped to make lowriders popular.

Ruben Gonzales inherited a well-worn pickup from his father. He changed it into a hard-hitting, mad-hopping dance machine with a 12-battery hydraulic setup. Those who watched the redone truck jump, jerk, and jolt named it the *Wicked One*.

Some lowriders honor memories. *Dreaming of You* features art inspired by an individual who is important to the owner.

Hydraulic modifications were only the first of many Ruben made to the *Wicked One*. Altogether, the changes cost him about $50,000. His truck has a **chopped** top (chopping is customizing a car or truck by removing a few inches horizontally from the top of the vehicle, for example, by cutting through the windows and windshield), a **channeled** frame (channeling is customizing a car by removing a few inches horizontally from the middle of the vehicle, for example, cutting through the doors and fenders), and a custom, see-through truck bed. Purple velvet upholstery shows off hundreds of hand-cut mirrors. The entire undercarriage is chrome-plated and painted with candy-blue and purple flakes. Airbrushed pictures of dragons and wizards cover the door jambs, hood, dashboard, and tailgate. Rueben gets attention wherever he drives.

For some, lowriders honor memories. When Raul Tostado was 2 years old, his father was killed in the Vietnam War. When Raul turned 18, he received money left by his father, to be used as he pleased. He bought a 1995 Toyota Camry.

As Raul thought about how he wanted his car to look, he imagined a painting honoring his father. Raul wanted it to represent both the past and the present. The artist suggested a mural of Raul's father in heaven with Jesus surrounded by clouds, and war scenes in the background. "The part I liked best was the paint job on the car," Raul said. "It's chameleon. When you look at it from the front, you see green. From the back, it seems purple. Looking at it straight on from the side, it looks yellow. I decided the color changes represent Vietnam flashbacks. If Dad had lived through the war, he would probably be having flashbacks like other soldiers do now. The car is really cool."

Raul named his car *Memories of War*. Raul says, "I'll keep working on it, like putting chrome on the undercarriage. I take it to car shows because I like to have people look at it. But I have deeper reasons. The car honors Dad. I want it to represent the war for all who were in Vietnam. Veterans who come by sometimes ask me about it, and I tell them my story."[18]

A lowrider is like a big canvas where owners tell about themselves. The interior represents the inside of themselves or their homes. The trim on the inside and the outside represents the owners' care and pride for their vehicles. As Little Willie G of Thee Midniters said in a song he wrote about Whittier Boulevard, "When you ride, that's how people know you; that's your identity."

5

GET TOGETHER IN CLUBS

When Spanish-speaking people moved from Mexico to California, they lived together in communities. They helped each other. As early as the 1930s, car owners cruised Whittier Boulevard in East Los Angeles. They stayed together, talked, and planned more cruises. The first lowrider club (before the word lowrider was used) might have been California's Thunderbolts. The members had cars with dropped suspension rather than speed equipment for racing. The hot rod's image was, "I'm fast, and I'm mean." The lowered customized car's image was, "I'm low, and I'm cool."

Throughout the years, car club members worked to bring a positive image to lowriders. Many clubs focused on lowriding as a healthy choice, away from gangs and drugs. Members take their cars to and tell their messages at schools. In fact, many of them tell future members that they won't be allowed into a car club if they use drugs or are in a gang.

Members of Española's Classic Creations, for instance, are required to sign a contract. They promise to stay away from drinking and drugs. If they break the rules, they are out of the club.

Mario de Alba (standing third from the right), immigrant from Mexico and founder of the Elite lowrider club, poses with his family at the Lowrider Experience car show in Los Angeles, California, in 2003. Three generations of the Alba family are lowriders, with the youngest dedicated to lowrider bicycles.

Car club members meet regularly for afternoon and evening cruises. They gather at parks or parking lots. They line up wagon-train fashion, and begin their slow-going caravan along city streets, around village plazas, and out onto country roads. Unlike hot rodders who traveled as fast as possible, lowriders go as slow as they can. They want to be seen (paint, chrome, low to the ground), and heard (stereos playing).

Victor Garcia started the Chicano Playaz Club, which admits only lowrider cars and trucks. Each owner and each vehicle must apply for membership. The club votes on the vehicle as well as its owner. "We take in winners," says Victor, "no dents, no rust. It must be nice. For example, when our

Any vehicle with wheels has the potential to be a lowrider. This baby was born into a lowrider family, so, naturally, he is starting out in a lowrider stroller.

club takes 18 entries to a car show, we usually come home with 17 winners. We're known as the 'picky club.'"[19]

This is a serious club. To be a full member of the Chicano Playaz Club, members must have made four major changes to their vehicles. Tinted windows, customized paint, stereo systems, and interior modifications all count. Adding murals anywhere on the vehicle also counts. Members also must have installed a hydraulic setup or intend to do so in the near future. "We have a good name," Victor explains. "No drugs, no gangs. We host car shows, and we judge car shows. Others who want to put on successful car shows pay us to use our name. We give the money we make to charity functions and sponsor school projects."[20]

There is a strong family feeling among car club members. Children sit alongside their parents during a club cruise. Many boys and girls will have lowered their bicycles and added new paint and chrome. Club members and their families get together for weekend picnics and camping trips. The lowrider tradition is passed on from father to son, aunt to niece, uncle to nephew, brother to brother or sister, husband to wife. Like other treasured family possessions, lowriders become heirlooms passed down through generations. For many families, lowriding is more than a hobby, it is a main part of their lives.

How does it feel to be the largest lowrider club in the world? "That's not our goal," answers Jae Brattain, the Uso Club's chief executive officer. "We like to win, but that's not our goal either."[21]

The car club *Uso* takes its name from the word that means "brothers—very close brothers"—in the language of the Samoan people. Samoa is a nation of nine islands in the South Pacific Ocean. Kita Lealao and some close friends from Samoa started the club in October 1992 in the harbor area of Los Angeles. The group chose tough guidelines. It would be family-oriented, but more importantly, people of any race or color could join. The club's major goal is to make groups of "brothers" throughout the club network, just as the name says.

In 1997 and 2004, *Lowrider* magazine named Uso the Car Club of the Year. Twenty-two club chapters quickly expanded to 40, including groups in Alaska, Hawaii, Guam, and Sweden. "We have a main set of rules, but we are flexible," Kita said. "As long as the clubs follow the bylaws by keeping the name in good stature, that's all we ask of them. As long as you love the game of lowriding, that's all that should matter."[22]

This young teen sits on his decorated and lowered bicycle at the annual lowrider car show at Kearny Park in Fresno, California. Family oriented activities of lowrider clubs have done much to overturn the negative impressions that were once associated with lowriders.

Uso members must act honorably and treat each other as brothers. The cars must be just as impressive: wire wheels only, clean at all times, and new improvements every 3 months. Unlike many car clubs, Uso's success has been 90 percent "person," or owner, and 10 percent "lowrider." The vehicle is important, but most important is the brother who belongs to the Uso family.

Uso has recently changed its name to Uce Car Clubs. The word Uso was too similar to the United Service Organization,

only a few members make an outstanding car club?

Twenty-five years after its founding in 1975, Thee Individuals Car Club is one of the most famous in the United States. Once a club of 26 members, Thee Individuals now has only four. Thee Individuals held their first annual Fresno car show in 1977. The show has been held every year since. "By now, we average 500 cars and 10,000 people," Pete Martinez said.*

Of the four members, three are named Martinez. Pete and Louis are brothers; Don Martinez is a longtime family friend. The fourth member is another longtime friend, Paul Avila.

When the club began, members went to a Los Angeles shop to have a plaque made. The shop had made a plaque—Thee Individuals—for another club whose members separated because of disagreements. "We didn't choose our name," Pete says. "It chose us, and we bought

(Continued...)

which serves military personnel. Uce is a shortened version of Uso. It still refers to the sacred bond between brothers.

Most car clubs and their members are responsible people, working toward honorable goals. Some clubs, however, do use lowriders as a cover for drug activity or forming gangs. For anyone who wants to find a car club to join, members of the clubs discussed in this book advise carefully checking out each club. Ask questions, listen to the answers, and it on sale. We trademarked and patented the name for our use only."**

Pete, the club's president, is proud of the club's history and its dedication to quality shows for every member of the family. As Pete describes it, "Young ones bring their bicycles and model cars to show. They learn about paints and patience and keeping their wheels clean. They're starting a hobby that keeps them involved in positive things."**

Thee Individuals' goal is to change the negative stereotype of the lowrider. If lowriders once were viewed as people with fancy cars but no jobs, now they are seen as supporters of the community, members of close families, and talented artists. "Anywhere we go, people know us," Pete says. "We are proud of our track record. We grow with our cars."**

*Ann Parr's telephone interview Pete Martinez, January 8, 2005.

**Ann Parr's telephone interview Pete Martinez, November 28, 1999.

watch members to make good choices. Ask for statements of a club's goals, ask how the club uses its money, and find out what a club does in the community. The best lowriders want a beautiful car. They use lowriding as a way to build family togetherness, encourage strong friendships, and build their communities.

6

LOWRIDERS OF TODAY

In some parts of the country, lowriding stays the same. Owners in the lower Southwest, for instance, remember family, religion, and Southwest landscapes when they decorate their cars. Their cars will be passed from one generation to the next. Lowriders from New Mexico are known as the lowest and slowest.

In other areas, lowriding means change. From the time the Chicano Movement began on Whittier Boulevard until today, many lowrider trends started in California. One of their early ideas was the scraper. Cars with small metal blocks welded to the back bumpers scraped the streets. Sparks flew. Quarter mile races showed who could scrape the lowest and the longest. Ray Aguirre's experiment with hydraulic setups began in California, too. That idea became popular and spread to other parts of the country. Flashy paint and fantasy designs caught owners' eyes. **Frenching** and **suicide** doors added more changes. (Frenching is installing handles, an antenna, headlights or taillights, or any other part below a vehicle's body to give a smooth look, with nothing protruding above the surface. Suicide doors are made by reversing the openings on doors, hoods, and trunks.) When California lowriders thought ideas and building skills could come together, they experimented.

This 1964 Chevy Impala rests on three wheels at the 2003 Lowrider Experience in Los Angeles, California. The car's hydraulics and chromed undercarriage are reflected in a mirror that is positioned underneath the car.

The latest California trend is to buy all-wheel-drive sport–utility vehicles (SUVs) and vans—the bigger the better—and put them down. "The Chevrolet Tahoe, Cadillac's Escalade, GMC's Yukon and Envoy Denali, and Ford's Expedition are popular choices," Nathan Trujillo said. "You'll see 24-to 26-inch rims on them at the shows, and expensive tires to match."[23] Nathan is features editor for *Lowrider* magazine.

Big wheels, not small ones, show off these large cars. Owners want them lowered, too. Master Image Customs has designed an air-suspension system that puts the vehicle down without interfering with the all-wheel drive. "A few years ago, owners wanted the cheapest parts and the cheapest labor," manager Adam Diaz said. "They're over that. Now they want bigger wheels with a lowered body. My largest customer base is Japan. They import the big SUVs and vans, and they want my product. In my opinion, Japan has become today's real trend-setter."[24]

Lowriding stays strong in Texas. Texas is *Lowrider* magazine's second largest market area. "They are willing to make their cars nearly undrivable," Nathan said. "They change their cars for design, not performance. They modify all the dynamics of the car they can until it does not come back together for a good drive. When compared with a sleek, high-performance car from California, the Texas car tends to win shows because of the radical changes. The California car may be the better product."[25]

By the early 1970s, women working on their own cars were accepted into the lowrider world. Many clubs had female members. Some clubs were for women only. Most top clubs, however, were for men only. Men were not sure women had the knowledge and money to make a contribution. A few women faced those hurdles anyway and began showing their cars. Sandra Velo's 1971 Buick Riviera won at shows in the early 1980s. "They had problems with a woman beating them in certain categories, like best chrome, best hydraulics, best 1970s custom, and almost always, best paint," Sandra said.[26]

By the late 1970s, even the most popular clubs began to accept women. "Lowriding is just a way of showing what you can really do," explained a member of Lady's Touch Car Club of Stockton, California. "It's something you work really hard for. It's a wonderful feeling."[27]

"Wives, girlfriends, and female car owners make up a small percentage of the lowriders we know about at *Lowrider* magazine," Nathan Trujillo said. "We consider them a vital part of the scene."[28]

A biker shifts his lowrider motorcycle into gear as he cruises Main Street in Daytona Beach, Florida, before an admiring crowd during Bike Week in March 2005.

By the mid-1970s, when lowriding was well known, Sonny Madrid and a couple of friends at San Jose City College made plans to publish newspapers or magazines. They wanted to tell people about the Chicano Movement. They promoted political rallies, dances, and events where they took pictures of cars. Lowrider owners, who had never seen their cars in print, wanted more. Soon, Sonny and his friends had enough money to start the next big project: *Low Rider* magazine. "The popular image of *la Chicanada* (Chicanos) has yet to be televised, written, or published," Sonny said. "The United States and the world has yet to discover the ***gente*** (folk)

Did you know

Kat Morris, a car builder and dealership owner, had the largest export business to Japan during the 1990s?

By the age of 17, she managed 103 employees in her California car-customizing business. She built 400 customized cars, most of which went to Japan. She believes in the lowrider movement. "Today's younger Hispanic generation goes one of two ways," she said. "Some who have money or can get money customize an SUV—put big wheels on it and have something that is no longer a straight street car. Or, they find a small Honda and put little wheels and chrome pipes on it and do primer paint. There's not much room for the in-between car anymore. Lowrider shows are for professionals—those who can sink $100,000 into a car.

"My opinion is that lowriders [have a new focus]," Kat continued. "Most of the parts are made in China. Only people with money can compete in the really big shows. But I don't think that's bad news. It may mean Hispanics have made their point and don't need lowriding to tell us who they are. Anyone, anywhere, with any amount of money can build a lowrider any way that they want."*

*Ann Parr's telephone interview with Kat Morris, December 8, 2004.

called Chicanos, especially the younger generation known as lowriders."[29]

Sonny and his team worked hard. By January 1977, they had hand-delivered 1,000 copies of the first issue of *Low Rider* magazine. Many were against the new magazine.

They thought lowriders meant violence and gangs. Law officers tried to stop Sonny's efforts. Scheduling more events for lowriders became almost impossible. But Sonny and his friends stuck with their dream.

By the end of 1979, *Low Rider* magazine had become the most successful Chicano publication in U.S. history. Sonny set up headquarters in East Los Angeles where he was close to famous car clubs. The NBC television network showed a special on *Low Rider* magazine and the cruising scene. Millions of people nationwide saw the lowriders of East Los Angeles.

Word spread that lowrider shows were exciting; they were not about violence and crime. By the 1980s, Sonny and his group held events all across the country. Successful national lowrider shows boosted the popularity of *Low Rider* magazine. They also provided photographs and stories for every issue.

Some say *Low Rider* magazine did not keep up with the latest trends and lowrider activities. Whatever the reasons, by 1982, the magazine was in trouble. Some staff people quit. Sales were down. The struggle continued, and in December 1985, *Low Rider* magazine shut down.

In the meantime, lowriding moved forward. Higher-quality cars showed up at shows, and minitrucks became popular. By October 1987, Alberto Lopez and Larry Gonzalez bought all rights to the old *Low Rider* magazine. The first issue of the redone magazine came out in June 1988, now called *Lowrider* (one word) magazine. All copies sold immediately. By the third issue, three times more readers bought the new magazine than had bought the old one. By 1990, *Lowrider* magazine was more successful than ever. Spin-offs—*Lowrider Arte*, *Lowrider Bicycle*, and *Lowrider Euro*—soon followed.

Lowriding is about attitudes, cultural expression, and transforming a car or any wheeled-vehicle in a way that says something about the owner's personality.

"I've always looked at lowriding as an art form, as cultural expression," explained Alberto Lopez. "I try to put as much into the magazine as a lowrider puts into his vehicle. . . . That comes from pride within."[30] By the early 2000s, readers in more than 50 countries were buying the magazine.

Some say lowriding has a predictable cycle. Owners spend money on their cars and shows until they are nearly broke. Then they take time to build up their bank accounts and return to their lowriders. Overall, in the early 1980s, nothing could stop the lowrider movement. People from

Chicago, Hawaii, and Sweden brought their cars to shows. Modern cars from California and the Southwest lowriders beat out their competition. Then lowrider activity slowed from 1986 to 1990. Beginning in 1987, lowrider minitrucks became popular. They were less expensive than big cars. Today, many lowriders who bought their cars as teens have matured into adults. They have more money. "I've got attorneys in my club," New Wave president Roberto Hernandez said. "We've got electricians, mail carriers, and people who work for the gas company. These people did something."[31] Lowrider owners seldom leave cruising behind.

No matter what their age, lowrider owners share a common excitement that keeps them going. They look at something with wheels—cars, trucks, motorcycles, bicycles, and tricycles. They look again and think about what could be changed that says something about who they are. They and their vehicles become one. As owners change over time, they change their cars, too.

Lowrider owners know what it takes to turn a crumpled-up junker into a shiny, smooth ride that turns heads. They know why they love lowriding. It is about attitudes and beliefs, and drama on the street. Lowriders are proud when they transform a hand-me-down car (or a new one) into a "looker."

Lowrider vehicles are about their owners. Solid, stable, and crouched down, hugging the ground, lowriders are ready to spring into action at the flick of a switch. They hop, buck, and kick to show that they are trying something new and reaching high. They settle down to hug the ground again to be in touch with their roots. They repeat the tradition when a decorated horse and rider were one. Lowrider and owner are one.

NOTES

Chapter 1

1. Ann Parr's telephone interview with Dennis Chavez, November 16, 2004.

2. Ann Parr's telephone interview with Patrick Chavez, November 20, 2004.

3. Ibid.

4. Carmella Padilla, *Low'n Slow* (Santa Fe, NM: Museum of New Mexico Press, 1999), 16–17.

5. Ann Parr's telephone interview with Tomas Martinez, November 17, 2004.

6. Ann Parr's telephone interview with Dennis Chavez, November 22, 1999.

7. Ann Parr's telephone interview with Patrick Chavez, November 20, 2004.

Chapter 3

8. Ann Parr's telephone interview with Tim Lona, January 11, 2005.

9. Ann Parr's telephone interview with Tim Lona, November 8, 2005.

10. Paige Penland, *Lowrider History, Pride, Culture* (St. Paul, MN: MBI Publishing-Motorbooks International, 2003), 16.

11.   Ibid., 19.

12.   Ann Parr's telephone interview with Dennis Chavez, October 10, 1999.

13.   Ann Parr's telephone interview with Adam Diaz, November 23, 2004.

Chapter 4

14.   Victoria Loe, "According to custom: shining example of lowrider to be part of NM cultures exhibit at Smithsonian," *Dallas Morning News*, June 2, 1992.

15.   Ann Parr's telephone interview with Dr. Benito Cordova, November 15, 2004.

16.   Victoria Loe, "According to custom: shining example of lowrider to be part of NM cultures exhibit at Smithsonian."

17.   Susannah Cassedy, "The High Art of Lowriding," *Museum News*, July/August 1992, 29.

18.   Ann Parr's telephone interview with Raul Tostado, October 21, 1999.

Chapter 5

19.   Ann Parr's personal interview with Victor Garcia, December 10, 1999.

20.   Ann Parr's telephone interview with Victor Garcia, December 17, 2004.

21. Ann Parr's telephone interview with Jae Brattain, November 29, 1999.

22. Jessica Lopez, "How to Start a Car Club," *Lowrider* magazine, April 2002, 43.

Chapter 6

23. Ann Parr's telephone interview with Nathan Trujillo, December 22, 2004.

24. Ann Parr's telephone interview with Adam Diaz, November 23, 2004.

25. Ann Parr's telephone interview with Nathan Trujillo, December 22, 2004.

26. Penland, *Lowrider History, Pride, Culture*, 44.

27. Ibid., 45.

28. Ann Parr's telephone interview with Nathan Trujillo, December 22, 2004.

29. Penland, *Lowrider History, Pride, Culture*, 74.

30. Ibid., 75.

31. Ibid., 113.

CHRONOLOGY

800–1500 Moors (an Islamic nomadic people from the northern shores of Africa) spread to Spain. The capital of Spain, Cordova, is the intellectual center of Europe.

1500–1810 The Aztec Indian Empire covers most of central and southern Mexico. Aztecs report that bearded white men, dressed in leather shields, carrying iron spears and crosses, have landed on the shores of the Gulf of Mexico. The strangers ride animals that snort and bellow, and when they run, the animals made a loud noise, as if stones were raining on the earth. Spain conquers Mexico, calling it New Spain, and introduces Catholicism to its inhabitants.

1810–1910 Mexico gains independence from Spain.

1846–1848 Mexican-American War begins because of a disagreement about where the line for the southern border of Texas should be drawn. The United States also wants to purchase the Mexican territories of California and New Mexico.

1863 New Mexico is divided in half. Territory of Arizona is created.

1910–1920 Until his murder in 1913, Francisco Madera leads Mexico toward democracy. With the Mexican Revolution, many Mexicans flee to their former land—California, New Mexico, and Arizona.

1940–1950 Mexican Americans customize their cars and clothes to preserve and display their Mexican culture.

1960–1990 Cars known as lowriders cruise the streets in California, New Mexico, Texas, and Arizona. Ray Aguirre makes the first hydraulic setup for his 1975 Corvette. He could raise and lower the height of his car so that he could drive it legally on normal streets.

1990–2005 Any person of any race or ethnicity can be a lowrider. Any car, truck, motorcycle, bicycle, tricycle, or model car can be lowered and customized to become a lowrider.

2005 The trend is to lower and customize big sport utility vehicles (SUVs) and large vans. Lowriders are found all over the world.

GLOSSARY

Altzan   The Aztec Indian word for "land of the blue herons," used by Mexican Americans in reference to the land acquired by the United States during the Mexican-American War. Altzan contains parts of present day Texas, California, and New Mexico.

Channeling   Customizing a car or truck by removing a few inches horizontally from the middle of the vehicle (making the vehicle shorter in length). For example, channeling can be done by cutting through the doors and fenders.

Cholos   The Spanish word for Mexican gangsters.

Chopping   Customizing a car or truck by removing a few inches horizontally from the top of the vehicle (making the vehicle shorter in length). For example, chopping can be done by cutting through the windows and windshield.

Caballeros   The Spanish word for horsemen.

Frenching   Further customizing a lowrider by installing handles, an antenna, headlights, taillights, or any other part below a vehicle's body to give it a smooth look—nothing protruding above the surface.

Gente   The Spanish word for folk.

Hop   How high a car can jump.

Uso   The Samoan word for very close brothers.

Pauchuco   The Spanish word for the best lowrider. *Pauchuco* means the ultimate "cool" and is a great compliment.

Sport Utility Vehicle (SUV)   An SUV is also known as an off-roader. It is a passenger vehicle which combines the load-hauling and passenger-carrying capacity of a large station wagon or minivan with features designed for off-road driving.

Suicide   Customizing a lowrider by reversing the openings on doors, hoods, and trunks.

FURTHER READING

Dunnington, Jacqueline Orsini. *Celebrating Guadalupe*. Tucson, AZ: Rio Nuevo Publishers, 2004.

Felson, Henry Gregor, ed. *Here is Your Hobby—Car Customizing*. New York, NY: G.P. Putnam's Sons, 1965.

Genat, Robert. *Lowriders*. St Paul, MN: MBI Publishers, 2001.

Hamilton, Frank. *How to Build a Lowrider*. North Branch, MN: CarTech, 1996.

Lake, E.D. *Lowriders*. Minneapolis, MN: Capstone Press, 1995.

Lowrider magazine, ed. *The Lowrider's Handbook*. New York, NY: HPBooks, 2002.

Parr, Danny. *Lowriders*. Mankato, MN: Capstone Press-Capstone High-Interest Books, 2002.

———. *Lowriders*. Philadelphia, PA: Chelsea House Publishers, 2001.

Perry, Michael. *Daniel's Ride*. San Francisco, CA: Free Will Press, 2001.

Werther, Scott P. *Lowriders*. New York, NY: PowerKids Press, 2002.

BIBLIOGRAPHY

"*1964 Civil Rights Act.*" History Learning Site.co.uk, May 2002. *www.historylearningsite.co.uk/1964_civil_rights_act.htm.*

"The 1965 Watts Riots." Sources for the Study of the 1965 Watts Riots. *www.usc.edu/isd/archives/la/watts.html.*

Cassedy, Susannah. "The High Art of Lowriding." *Museum News*, July/August 1992.

Dunnington, Jacqueline Orsini. *Viva Guadalupe!* Santa Fe, NM: Museum of New Mexico Press, 1997.

Garcia, Anne. "Lowriders Ride High in Española." *American Profile*, April 29, 2001–May 5, 2001. *http://americanprofile.com/issues/20010429/20010429cen_794.asp.*

Lenchek, Shep. "The Aztecs Speak: An Aztec Account of the Conquest of Mexico." Mexico Connect, 2005. *www.mexconnect.com.*

Loe, Victoria. "According to custom: shining example of lowrider to be part of NM cultures exhibit at Smithsonian." *Dallas Morning News*, June 2, 1992.

Lopez, Jessica. "How to Start a Car Club." *Lowrider* magazine, April 2002.

"Mexican-American War." *Mexican-American War—Wikipedia, the free encyclopedia*, June 28, 2005. *http://en.wikipedia.org/wiki/Mexican-American_War*.

MexOnline staff. "The Mexican Revolution of 1910." MexOnline.com, April 2004. *www.mexonline.com/revolution.htm*.

Moors. Encyclopedia.com. *www.encyclopedia.com/html/m/moors.asp*.

Padilla, Carmella. *Low 'n Slow*. Santa Fe, NM: Museum of New Mexico Press, 1999.

Palfrey, Dale Hoyte. "The Post-Classic Period (900–1521 AD)—Part 2: The Aztecs." Mexico Connect, 1997. *www.mexconnect.com*.

Penland, Paige. *Lowrider History, Pride, Culture*. St. Paul, MN: MBI Publishing-Motorbooks International, 2003.

Serrano, Francisco. *Our Lady of Guadalupe*. Toronto, Ontario: Groundwood Books, 1998.

Smithsonian Collection. " 'Dave's Dream' Lowrider." America on the Move | "Dave's dream" lowrider. *www.americanhistory.si.edu/onthemove/collection/object_1187.html*.

"Time Line Overview." Mexico Connect, 2005. *www.mexconnected.com/cgi-bin/community/community.cgi?url=http%3A%2F%2Fmexconnected.com%2F%2Findex.html*.

"Timeline of New Mexico History." *PPSA* magazine, January 8, 2000. *www.ppsa.com/magazine/NMtimeline.html.*

Tuck, Jim. "Glorious Innocent: The Tragedy and Triumph of Francisco Ignacio Madero." Mexico Connect, 1999. *www.mexconnect.com.*

"The Virgin of Guadalupe." Casa Mexicana, March 3, 2005. *www.casamexicanafolkart.com/the_virgin_of_guadalupe.html.*

"Watts Riots." *Watts riots—Wikipedia, the free encyclopedia*, July 6, 2005. *http://en.wikipedia.org/wiki/Watts_Riots.*

INTERNET SITES

http://en.wikipedia.org

> *This site is an online encyclopedia where information about the Mexican-American War, the Watts Riots in California, and Chimayó, New Mexico, can be found.*

www.americanhistory.si.edu

> *This is the official site for the American History Museum of the Smithsonian Institution. Information about "Dave's Dream," a famous lowrider on exhibit can be found here.*

www.americanprofile.com

> *This is the website for a weekly four-color magazine that celebrates hometown American life. Read about Española, New Mexico, here.*

www.casamexicanafolkart.com

> *Information about The Virgin of Guadalupe can be found on this site.*

www.encyclopedia.com

> *This site is a general online encyclopedia, easy to search, and complete in their answers.*

www.lowridermagazine.com

> *This is the official site for the largest Chicano publication and the most extensive site for lowriders.*

www.mexconnect.com

This site provides facts about Mexican history, including information about the Aztec Indians. You must be a member to search articles.

www.mexonline.com

This is an online guide to Mexico's history, activities, and culture.

www.ppsa.com/magaine.NMtimeline.html

This is an online magazine. You can search for articles from their archives.

www.ucefamily.com

This is the official site for the Uso/Uce Car Club, the largest in the world.

Photo Credits:

INDEX

ABOUT THE AUTHOR

Ann Parr, a freelance writer and former elementary school teacher, lives with her husband in Lindsborg, Kansas, a quiet little Swedish community. When she is not writing, she may be fulfilling business consulting assignments with her husband, jogging, playing the piano or organ, or visiting children and grandchildren. She recently completed her Master's of Fine Arts Degree in Writing for Children from Vermont College. She writes children's books and magazine articles, often about sports and sports figures. She likes cars and remembers a time when she could identify the make and model of most any car going up and down the highways. She also remembers learning to drive her dad's 1950 stick shift, dead-green Chevrolet pickup truck. She appreciates lowriders for their dedication to beauty and family.